Wish You 1

AT

EXMOUTH

GEORGE PRIDMORE

OBELISK PUBLICATIONS

OBELISK PUBLICATIONS specialise in books about Devon. We have developed a range of titles which cover such themes as nostalgia, strange and spooky stories, books about walking and books about specific locations. We aim to produce titles which will interest anyone who has a love of Devon. Some of our titles are:

Around & About the Haldon Hills, Chips Barber
The Lost City of Exeter, Chips Barber
Adventure Through Red Devon, Raymond B. Cattell
An Exeter Boyhood, Frank Retter
Under Sail Through South Devon & Dartmoor, R. B. Cattell
Ide, Bill Rowland
Diary of a Devonshire Walker, Chips Barber
Rambling in the Plymouth Countryside, Woolley & Lister
The Great Little Dartmoor Book, Chips Barber
The Great Little Exeter Book, Chips Barber
Memories of Newton Abbot, Elsie Townsend
Albert Labbett's Crediton Collection
TV and Films Made in Devon, Chips Barber & David FitzGerald
Dartmoor in Colour, Chips Barber
Burgh Island & Bigbury Bay, Chips Barber & Judy Chard
Dark & Dastardly Dartmoor, Sally & Chips Barber
Talking About Topsham, Sara Vernon
An Alphington Album, Aplin and Gaskell
Tales of the Unexplained in Devon, Judy Chard
Exeter in Colour, Chips Barber
Torbay in Colour, Chips Barber
Haunted Happenings in Devon, Judy Chard
The Dawlish Collection, Bernard Chapman
The Totnes Collection, Bill Bennett
Walking with a Tired Terrier In and Around Torbay, Brian Carter
The Ghosts of Exeter, Sally & Chips Barber
The Ghosts of Torbay, Deryck Seymour
The Ghosts of Berry Pomeroy Castle, Deryck Seymour
The Great Little Totnes Book, Bill Bennett
Tales of the Teign, Chips Barber & Judy Chard
Ten Family Walks on Dartmoor, Sally & Chips Barber
Torquay United – the First 70 Years, Laura Joint
The A to Z of Dartmoor Tors, Terry Bound

If you would like further details of currently available titles, please send an s.a.e. to the address given below or telephone (0392) 68556.

Picture on bottom of page 18 reproduced by kind permission of Pamlin Cards, Croydon

First published in 1991 by
Obelisk Publications, 2 Church Hill, Pinhoe, Exeter, Devon
Designed by Chips and Sally Barber
Edited and Typeset by Sally Barber
Printed in Great Britain by Penwell Print Ltd, Callington, Cornwall

© George Pridmore 1991
All Rights Reserved

Wish You Were Here ... at Exmouth

"Having a good time" ... "Weather is fine" ... "Wish you were here".

Such comments as these have been appearing regularly on picture postcards dropping into letter boxes all over the country for years.

As the annual holiday became a recognised feature of everyday life – originally just a week or a fortnight at the seaside – so the sending of postcards became an accepted part of those holidays.

Those left at home – relatives, neighbours, friends and work colleagues – came to expect them. A card might even be sent to the boss, but this would probably not include the "wish you were here" reference.

Messages on the cards followed a fairly routine pattern – details of the journey to the holiday destination; the weather; the accommodation and food; and what the sender has been doing.

As the postcard sending tradition expanded into a profitable business, the types on sale in shops fell into three main categories – the view card, the novelty card, and the comic card, although the latter usually had no printed reference to the resort concerned.

This book gives some examples of tall three types of card which have been sent by people staying at one lovely and popular seaside resort in Devon since the turn of the century. And who knows? Maybe as you glance through its pages, you will get a feeling of – wishing you were here, at Exmouth.

The card below is part of one of the few postcards which were actually published in Exmouth – by Henry John Appleby who ran a stationery business in The Strand.

The most popular place for taking a photograph for a view postcard of Exmouth seems to be where the Esplanade joins Morton Crescent and Alexandra Terrace. Cards showing this area from various angles are profuse. This is an early example, sent in 1903. The view includes some notable Exmouth landmarks – the Clock Tower, built to commemorate Queen Victoria's Diamond Jubilee; the Gentlemen's Club (now the Elizabeth Hall), the historic row of houses on the Beacon; Holy Trinity Church; and the Imperial Hotel.

The first postcard a holidaymaker often sends on reaching the chosen holiday destination is to advise those at home – "have arrived safely".

A close view of the bathing machines and a picture which emphasises the respectability and propriety which was expected on the beach in the earlier days of this century. Not a swim suit or partly dressed sun-bather in sight.

In the 1920s topless bathing was prohibited for both sexes. It was apparently still unseemly even to sunbathe in a swim suit.

In the distance can be seen boats ready for that other customary attraction of a seaside holiday – "a trip around the bay" – which really meant, in the case of Exmouth, a trip along the coast to Sandy Bay.

The picture above shows the beach in the 1930s with a refreshment stall, complete with chairs and tables. The blackboard notice alongside the stall invites customers to try "Our Devonshire Cream Ices" – cornets and wafers at prices ranging from 1d to 4d. Also offered are "Iced Drinks 4d and 6d". On the extreme left is a "Fishpond" amusement stall while on the beach beyond that can be seen a children's roundabout.

Both the cards below are from the early 1930s. The right hand one is of the novelty pull-out variety with a flap which lifts up to reveal a strip of 12 small photographs of Exmouth. Both emphasise the "wish you were here" theme.

Misprints sometimes appear on postcards – like this one showing the entrance to the Docks and what is described as the "Starecross" Launch. This should, of course, read "Starcross". At one time it was an all-the-year-round ferry, connecting with trains on the old GWR line between Exeter and South Devon. This card, sent in 1913, also shows the Pavilion on the Pier, which held 500 people and was used for many years for concerts and similar events.

Here is another view of the Pier and its Pavilion. Besides providing a centre of entertainment and amusement, the Pier, which was constructed in the 1860s, was used by the pleasure steamers which sailed between various Devon resorts. During its lifetime it has also housed a skating rink, a fun-fair, a roundabout, and an auto-scooter rink which claimed that you could: "Learn to drive your own car – 100 smiles an hour". This card, also dating from 1913, shows the Pier when it was possible to walk underneath it and when it was longer than it is now.

Two popular holiday attractions at Exmouth have been concert parties and donkeys. Both started on the sands, but the former then moved on to present their shows first in the Pier Pavilion, and then in the Manor Gardens. The photograph shows one of the earlier concert parties, a pierrot troupe called "The Coronet Entertainers". Meanwhile the novelty card sums up the pleasures of a donkey ride enjoyed by younger holiday makers.

And here's the real thing in donkey rides – a picture postcard dating from the 1930s. In the background some boatmen may be seen encouraging holiday makers to board their vessels for a "trip around the bay". For those who wished to venture further afield, the two pleasure steamers, *Duke of Devonshire* and *Duchess of Devonshire* are waiting, moored at the Pier head.

Above is another card from the 1930s and the days when beach huts were actually sited on the beach. And there was obviously no beach-ban on dogs in those days, as two of them may be seen enjoying sun and sand.

Below is a picture of the *Duchess of Devonshire* as she makes her way from the Pier with a load of passengers. But the main interest which Exmouth Pier held for the writer of this postcard, sent in September 1904, was not the comings and goings of the paddle steamers, nor even the free concerts advertised alongside the Pavilion. The message on the card simply says: "We have been on the pier trying the automatic machines."

Passengers who had their photographs taken on a steamer trip could, a day or two later, call on the photographer, F. H. Wilson at Camperdown Terrace, quote the appropriate number – 310 in this case – and collect copies in postcard form. The destinations included Torquay and Plymouth, while teas and luncheons could be enjoyed on board.

Another pleasure trip which was something of a holiday 'must' was a motor coach drive. This charabanc party of trippers are all ready to set out on a journey from Miller's Garage in The Strand, the premises now occupied by Exmouth Indoor Market.

Here's a couple who seem to be finding contentment in each other's company. This card was sent in 1913 when cycling was all the rage.

The card below was sent in 1917, by a young lady, to her soldier boyfriend, recalling the "nice time and cuddle" they had on the sands, comparing themselves to the couple in the picture.

The weather has frequently been the subject of the comic card – like these two sent from Exmouth in 1911 and 1918 respectively. However the sender of the umbrella card refuted the need for a "brolly" in Exmouth by writing "... it has been glorious sunshine ever since we arrived".

While most of the concerts given in the Manor Gardens were by military bands, a dance band was in residence there for a number of summer seasons in the late 1930s. What was particularly unusual was that the musicians were all female. Evelyn Hardy & her Ladies Band enjoyed a large following and fans could buy postcard photographs of the band, either to keep or to send to friends or relations. During one summer season Evelyn Hardy and her Band gave a BBC broadcast from the Manor Gardens, and the large crowds which it attracted caused severe traffic problems on nearby roads.

For a long time the Manor Gardens was a popular place to sit and listen to the band. Formerly part of the Manor House grounds, the Gardens were opened to the public in 1896 and its bandstand proved a major attraction with bands giving concerts up to three times a day during the holiday season. It is shown here on a card sent in August 1915.

Another Exmouth bandstand, which proved a popular rendezvous, was in the seafront gardens, opposite where the Pavilion now stands. Although the notice on the grass in the centre of the picture on this late 1920s postcard reads "Dancing is Prohibited", it was not unknown for couples to take their partners for a waltz or fox-trot from time to time.

This is not Watley Combe Church as stated on the card but the Church of St. John the Evangelist, the Parish Church of Withycombe! It was built in 1864 at a cost of £5,000 raised mainly by local subscriptions.

An attraction at Withycombe was the old mill, pictured here in August 1908. It was a victim of the disastrous floods which struck Exmouth in 1960. The wheel was preserved and is now at the end of Bath Road, opposite the Imperial Hotel.

The concert party of Ninon and "The Follies" spent several seasons in Exmouth, proving extremely popular. A 1950s holiday guide announced: "Your summer holiday is not complete without a visit to the Manor Grounds, Exmouth. See the Follies – famous throughout Devon, with a reputation second to none."

Some happy youngsters seem to have been learning the rudiments of driving – and maybe the Highway Code – when the photographer caught the above scene in the Children's Amusement Park in the 1950s.

Next we see Exmouth Golf Links which was sited on the Maer from 1866, when a local golf club was formed, and continued to be used until just after World War II. The former Club House later became Exmouth Zoo but now houses an amusement complex.

The former sea-front gardens also featured bowling greens as shown here on a postcard sent to London in 1915. A photograph taken from a similar spot today would show the Pavilion in the background instead of trees.

With the coming of the aeroplane, postcards with aerial views of holiday resorts began to appear in the shops. A card like the one below would be of particular interest to any holiday maker who took one of those short 5/- trips in a biplane. This postcard, dating from the early 1930s, shows the old Coastguard houses which stood alongside the lifeboat station and also the beach huts when they were actually situated on the beach.

For some people, the best kind of holiday was the camping kind – one spent in a tent, caravan, or a rather primitive chalet standing in a field. The Sandy Bay area of Exmouth became very popular for this type of holiday and this postcard shows Sandy Bay as it was just after the 1939/45 War – with just one cafe and a few caravans and chalets. It is difficult to reconcile this scene with the large popular holiday complex which occupies the same site nowadays.

Not far from Sandy Bay is the village of Littleham, a pretty spot. Featured on this postcard, dated 15 August 1917, this delightful, peaceful and rural setting was in stark contrast to the scenes being witnessed across the Channel in those days of World War I.

This is another view of Sandy Bay in the days when it was known as the Holiday Camp, West Down Farm, Littleham.

Before the motor car became popular, many people spending holidays in the Littleham or Sandy Bay area would go by train. So why not a postcard showing the station which is your destination? This is the former Littleham station as photographed from the down platform. The station was on the Exmouth-Budleigh Salterton-Tipton St. John line and was situated just off Cranford Avenue, on the site now occupied by Jarvis Close. The line was closed by British Rail under the "Beeching Axe" and the last passenger train called at Littleham Station on 4 March 1967.

Of course, if you stayed at one of the local hotels, it was sometimes possible to purchase a picture postcard of the actual establishment. This one shows the former Thorns Hotel in The Parade, described on the reverse of the card as: "The Thorns Hotel and Restaurant, BRTA, Commercial and Private, W. J. Pile, Proprietor. Tel. 99". This aerial photograph shows the proximity of the hotel to the railway station – the old station which was demolished in 1926 – and was taken in the days when it was operated by the London & South Western Railway Company.

Mrs Yate also seems to have produced her own postcard for her boarding establishment – No 2 San Remo, The Esplanade, a property forming part of a large sea-front hotel. Perhaps it was Mrs Yate herself who is pictured with another lady and a dog on the steps of San Remo.

In days gone by, J. Thorn issued a postcard which could be purchased and sent away by visitors so ensuring that his refreshment rooms on Exmouth Pleasure Grounds at The Maer would be well advertised.

Some visitors preferred to spend their holidays at one of the small buildings in the Shelly Beach and Docks area. These rather quaint properties have been variably described as "chalets", "bungalows" or, as on this 1910 card, "boathouses". They proved extremely popular for many years and some eventually became permanent homes. Most have since been demolished.

Another aerial photograph postcard, this time concentrating on the Docks area. Besides featuring such places as the pier and Shelly Beach, this picture clearly shows (top centre) the old railway line which ran from the station to the Dock basin.

Traditional holiday breakfast fayre was a pair of kippers and memories of a once popular expression, "as giddy as a kipper", are revived here by this card. It was sent by someone having "a lovely time" in 1911.

Some further examples of the novelty "pull-out" type of card each with strips of 12 small photographs of Exmouth under the flaps. Although the dates when the cards were sent vary from 1912 to 1924, the subjects of each are very similar. These included views of the beach, sea-front and pier, Holy Trinity Church, Manor Gardens, the Plantation and the old Town Hall in Rolle Street.

The most unusual one here must be the card shaped like a crab (opposite) with the message "just pinched a bit of Exmouth". Attached to the "crab" by a piece of thin red cord is a small luggage label to be used for sending it through the post.

SOUVENIR
OF
EXMOUTH

News and Views
from
Exmouth.

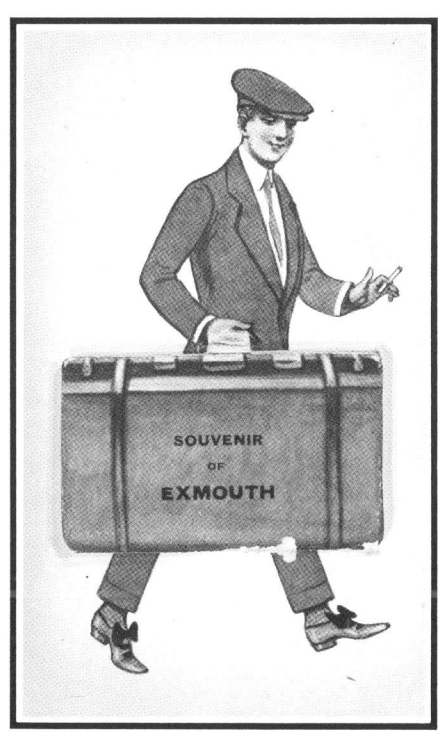

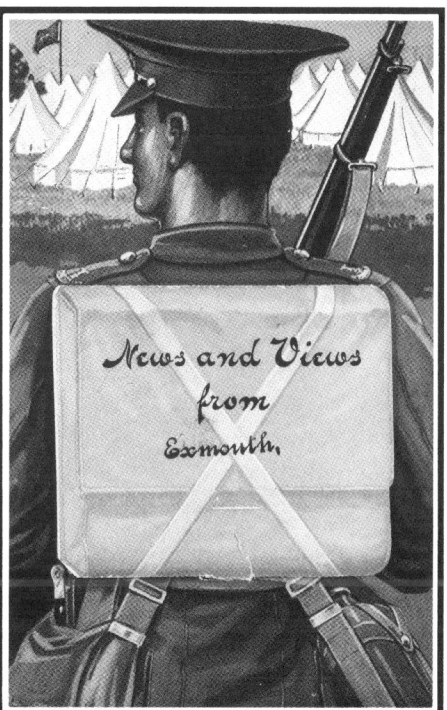

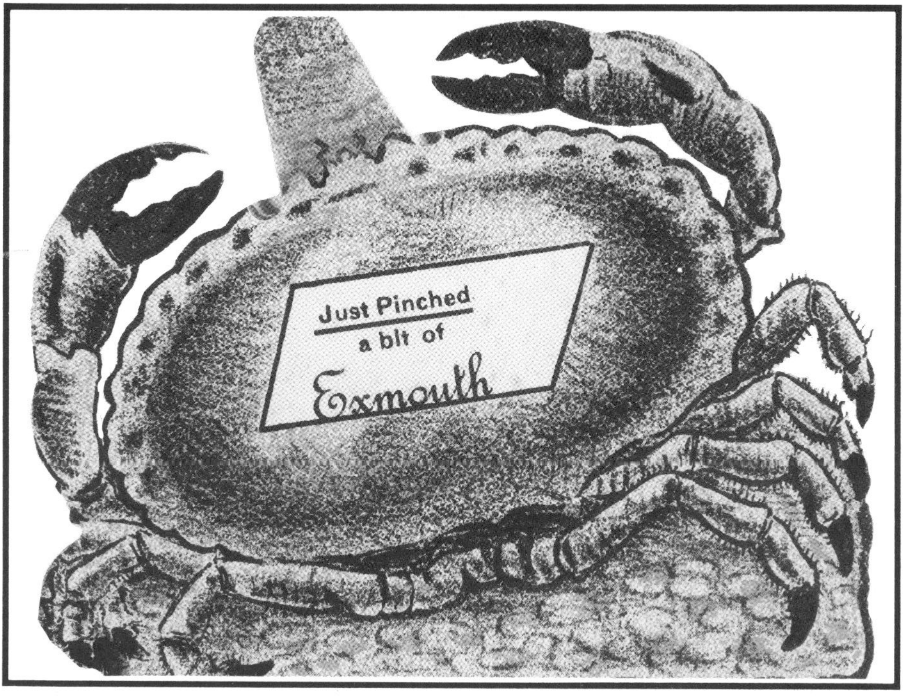
Just Pinched
a bit of
Exmouth

The above picture could hardly be described as a "Wish-you-were-here" card as it was sent by someone in Exmouth on business in September 1908. The message on the reverse reads: "Been to see a client down here. It's a lovely morning and hope to have a good time on the water this afternoon." It seems an appropriate card to send bearing in mind the anticipated boat trip. Maybe the trip involved a visit to Dawlish Warren from where this photograph, looking across towards Exmouth, was taken.

Below is a rare scene showing some quite substantial chalets on the beach near the former Coastguard Station. Just right of centre is the Coastguard look-out tower and on the far left is the building which is still a sea front cafe. This card was one of a booklet of twelve which could be taken out when required simply by tearing along the perforated edge.

Orcombe Point has always been a favourite rendezvous for some visitors and, as this card shows, there even used to be a refreshment hut on the beach there. Incidentally, this card, sent in 1927, also confirms that even day-trippers liked to send postcards. The message on the reverse begins: "Spending the day, and some money, at Exmouth."

To reach Orcombe Point these days there is a well-built promenade called Queen's Drive, with roadway, pavement and sea-wall. Queen's Drive looked quite different in 1909, as this postcard shows, but it still seems to have attracted a lot of visitors, particularly well-dressed young men and ladies.

Not every town has a coastguard station so this obviously used to be an ideal subject for a holiday picture postcard. The Exmouth Preventative (or Coastguard) Station was built on the seafront in the 1820s mainly to combat the smuggling traffic which was rife at that time. It incorporated houses for occupation by the men of the coastguard service and their families. The land where the station and houses was sited is now used for leisure purposes including a boating lake.

Sometime after the coastguard station was built, a lifeboat station was erected next to it, also a popular subject for a souvenir postcard. The lifeboat pictured on this card is the Catherine Harriet Eaton. It was built in 1932 and was stationed at Exmouth from 1933 to 1953.

Exmouth Council's Open-Air Pool, on the sea front, was opened in 1932 and served the town well for around half a century until an indoor pool was constructed at the new Council Sports Centre. The former pool has now been converted into a privately run fun pool complex.

Besides sitting on the beach, visitors like to do a bit of shopping. The Parade has been a popular shopping area over the years. Early in the 18th century, a prominent local resident, Sir John Colleton, built a raised gravel walk alongside the estuary which then extended to the area. In 1790 houses were built on the walk and eventually both sides of The Parade were developed with more houses and shops. This card shows The Parade as it was in 1911.

Around the corner from The Parade is The Strand, one of Exmouth's longest established areas. This was to be the scene of the worst bombing incident in the town during World War II when a bomb demolished the gable roofed premises on the left killing a number of people waiting for a bus outside the shops.

Exeter Road was for years the main road leading out of Exmouth. It was originally a turnpike or toll road. This postcard shows the road in 1928 with, in the distance, the railway bridge, carrying the old Exmouth-Budleigh Salterton branch line, which was demolished in 1981. With the opening of the new Marine Way by-passing the town, Exeter Road became a cul-de-sac. However a campaign and pressure from local residents led to its reopening.

Two more areas which have been favoured by shoppers over the years are Rolle Street and High Street. These postcards show them looking far more deserted than they ever are these days. Rolle Street was developed by the Lord of the Manor, Lord Rolle, in the 1860/70s to replace a congested area of buildings and small courts, and its first shop opened in 1863. High Street, leading from Rolle Street to Chapel Hill, has existed longer as a highway, but was rebuilt in 1875.

A special 'find' for a postcard sender would be one showing the holiday-maker's accommodation thus providing the opportunity to write on the card "x marks the spot where we are staying". Maybe that is why a cross was placed over a house in Victoria Road on this postcard sent in July 1909.

Featured in this 1922 postcard of Park Road is another bridge carrying the Budleigh Salterton branch line and part of the railway viaduct which was once a prominent Exmouth landmark. As the name of the road implies, it leads to Phear Park, the popular attraction for visitors which may be seen in the distance.

What the Girls at Exmouth have plenty of.

For a nice Spoon you cant beat EXMOUTH.

Back in those days of the 1914/18 war, when the expression 'to spoon' was an amorous term, Flo sent this novelty spoon card to her soldier boyfriend. On it she wrote: "Dear Fred, Do you think there is any truth in this card? I think a nice spoon at Exmouth is good. I don't think it could be bad anywhere with a nice boy." Her message seems to confirm the theory put forward by the other card, sent in 1913, that Exmouth girls have plenty of 'sauce'.

It's time to go home, and having sent a card to advise safe arrival at the start of the holiday, why not send one to announce departure at the end? Here's a most appropriate one for that purpose. It was sent by someone leaving Exmouth after a holiday in August 1907.

There was never a railway link between Exmouth and the nearby village of Withycombe (now a part of Exmouth) but this did not deter the publisher of this comic postcard from poking a bit of fun at the railway company.

We end our nostalgic journey through postcards of the past appropriately with one showing passengers boarding a train at Exmouth station in the days of the old London & South Western Railway, with the guard making his way along the platform with his green flag to give the train a send-off.